"HIP" Recollections of Darby Hicks

To Rick!
DIG DARBY
ENJOY
SIR. BOB-O

"HIP" Recollections of Darby Hicks

◆

(The Musings of a Senior Bronx Homeboy)

Poetically and Jazzfully Expressed by Bob Washington

iUniverse, Inc.
New York Lincoln Shanghai

"HIP" Recollections of Darby Hicks
(The Musings of a Senior Bronx Homeboy)

All Rights Reserved © 2003 by Bob Washington

No part of this book may be reproduced or transmitted in any form or by any means, graphic, electronic, or mechanical, including photocopying, recording, taping, or by any information storage retrieval system, without the written permission of the publisher.

iUniverse, Inc.

For information address:
iUniverse, Inc.
2021 Pine Lake Road, Suite 100
Lincoln, NE 68512
www.iuniverse.com

ISBN: 0-595-29362-X

Printed in the United States of America

Contents

- Acknowledgements vii
- *1922-1939 "HIP" Recollections POETICALLY Expressed* 1
- *1922-1939 Recollections JAZZFULLY Expressed* 7
- *1940-1949 "Hip" Recollections POETICALLY Expressed* 13
- *1940-1949 Recollections JAZZFULLY Expressed* 16
- *1950-1969 "Hip" Recollections POETICALLY Expressed* 22
- *1950-1969 Recollections JAZZFULLY Expressed* 26
- *1970-1979 "Hip" Recollections POETICALLY Expressed* 44
- *1980-1989 Recollections JAZZFULLY Expressed* 47
- *1990-Millenium "Hip" Recollections POETICALLY Expressed* 57

Acknowledgements

First and above all to my Wife Helen who had the "Stick-to-it-ness" through thick and thin. Love ya' Babe! And the same for our daughter, Valerie.

To the "Awesome 4SUM"; namely Ernie, Ham, Chubby, and me: Over fifty years of friendship I dug and was hard to beat.

To many, many other friends, (You know who you are), it's been a deep and profound "Expoobident" privilege to have had each one of you a part of my life.

Finally, to Charlie, a cat without whose technical and literary dexterity the journey of Darby Hicks could not have been accomplished. Mucho thanks, man!

1922-1939 "HIP" RECOLLECTIONS POETICALLY EXPRESSED

"Growin' Up"…"Standin' Up"…"Throwin' Up"
"Bread Lines"…"Clothes Lines"…"Shoe Shines"

In 1922 it became my turn.
To see the light. To begin to learn.
To give. To take. And to make my
journey through life, very cool.

Unraveling, like thread off a spool.
A piece of cake. Big mistake. Fool!
Like, when I was about three, the
Boogieman scared the shit outta me.

Now, I never saw the cat.
But, my Mama said it was a fact.
So, I had to accept that.
'Cause I found out early in my life.

Never question Daddy or his Wife
'Bout nothin' at all. Big or Small.
Like, takin' Castor Oil or Sassafras Tea.
Man, that stuff worked immediately.

It cleaned your teeth, straightened your hair.
Made you feel good, everywhere.

But, it kept my ass as slick as boiled okra.
And, burned it like a red hot poker.

"Don't get your feet wet", Mama said.
"Get whoopin' cough, you'll stay in bed".
The smell of Octagon Soap was prevalent.
The roach parade was always evident.

"Sleep tight"………………………
"Don't let the bedbugs bite"……
Stone Ghetto Bloodsuckas………
Mean Muthafuckas!!!…………………

I had a weak bladder.
So, my bed was always wet.
And you can bet, them bugs dug that scene.
Kept them fat…never lean.

Just couldn't get rid of them Bad Boys.
Tried Flint. Fire. Even Noise. Chicken feet
was the meat for homemade soup.
Hangin' out, was sittin' on the stoop.

Keepin' my knickers above my knees.
To remember to always say please.
Paying attention. Minding the Golden Rule.
Daddy's razor strop, was the learnin' tool.

Now, if you sucked your teeth, or rolled
your eyes. SURPRISE!
After you got up off the floor. You can bet
your ass, you didn't do that anymore.

A backhand lick from outta the blue.
All you could ask…"What'd I do"!
How could I forget my first day in school?
Picking my nose. Wiping the drool.

Day after day seeing new faces.
In all the different places.
Careful not to sass.
Writing two poems in my 3rd grade class:

"THE FLAG

See the Flag up in the air.
You see it almost everywhere.
Over Land. Over Sea.
Waving my Country Tis' of Thee.

CHRISTOPHER COLUMBUS

Christopher Columbus was a mighty man.
Sailed the ocean to discover this land.
He claimed the land in the honor of Spain.
But, Americus Vespucious gave it its name."

(Two {2} poems by Darby; Teacher: Ms. Lester
3rd Grade. P.S. 23 The Bronx 1930)

I began to wonder what else my middle
leg was for.
It had to be used for more, than writing
my name in the snow.

So, I asked my friend Moe. I knew he
would know. He straightened me out.
Told me all about the birds and bees.
CHEEZ!

And pickin' a fight with the baddest cat
I could find. I had to be outta my fuckin'
mind. He kicked my ass for days. 44 different
ways. Starting on Monday. Twice on Sunday.

But, you know somethin', Bro'.
Don't seem like it was too long ago.
We was "gettin' down" at the playground.
A game of basketball on the half court.

Without taking a snort.
Hell, who needed blow.
We got high on give-and-go.
Talkin' 'bout playin' hooky.

Gettin' some nooky.
How it sure was groovy.
Playin' "stink finger" with the chicks
in the movie.

Shining shoes to make some dough.
Had a problem with the cash flow.
You know?
That's the way it was. Cuz!

And hitching on a trolley car.
We didn't go far.
But, we got around.
Like, uptown.

Making a scooter outta old roller
skates. Without any brakes.
Ring-a-lee-vee-O was the game of
the day. Everybody wanted to play.

Stick ball. Punch ball. Kick the can.
Man!……………………
Who could forget. "Johnny on a pony"
123! Seems like the pony was always me.

Meet at the candy store after the game.
Munchin' on a Charlotte Russe.
While sippin' a "for two cents plain".
Boy, did we have fun, till the day was done.

But, when Mama called from the window
to come home. You best not roam.
And get home before Dad.
Or else your ass would be had.

Now Mama could deal with whatever.
But Dad……NEVER! EVER!
*"I works too hard…and I ain't got no
time for no mess"*…………

Now, I confess I knew just what he meant.
So I spent my time doing what was right.
Morning…Noon…Night.
Winter…Summer…Spring and Fall.

**AND YOU KNOW WHAT!………..
IT DID NOT HURT AT ALL!!………**

1922-1939 RECOLLECTIONS JAZZFULLY EXPRESSED

I recall, my father had a gig in the
Post Office. He worked nights. My mother
was always yelling at me and my sisters.
"Be quiet, your father is sleeping". She
had a broomstick, which she used to bang
on the ceiling. It was a signal for the cats
who lived over us, to cool with the stomping,
and running around.
She finally didn't have to do that
anymore. My father moved to a top floor
apartment. My father was always moving.
Especially, if he had to bang on the radiator
to get any heat. If the janitor skipped us with
the dumbwaiter on garbage day. The janitor
was always drunk. He skipped everybody.
I sure didn't dig living on the top floor.
I recall, I went to see the movie Frankenstein.
Going to the movies, was an all day affair. A
double feature, sometimes three movies.
Short subjects. Fox Movietone News, and a
chapter of a continuing serial.

So, when I got home, it was dark. I was
afraid to go upstairs. I just knew that
Boris Karloff, the monster was on the
roof waiting for me. My sisters had to
come down and get me. After that, they
started calling me, "scairdy cat".
The apartment houses on the

block where we lived, was attached. Me and a friend of mine, used to play a lot on the roof. It was like our own playground. We played hide and seek. Chased each other, as we jumped from roof to roof.
One day my friend brought his little dog up on the roof to play with us. The dog began jumping with us, from roof to roof. When we got to the last roof, the dog jumped for the next roof. I guess he thought it was attached. It wasn't. I'll never forget how I felt, as I watched him fall. It was a long time, before I went up on the roof again.
I recall, one day I was playing a game of association on the block. It was one of the favorite games I liked to play.

It was like football, except there was no tackling, or knocking somebody on their ass. It was all about passing the football. I couldn't catch the ball for shit, but I could throw a mean ass spiral. There was a cat on my team by the name of Frankie. He lived in the same building, as I did. Man, Frankie, could run his ass off. If you ever got into a race with Frankie, all you ever saw, was that cats heels. That brother, could motor. He ran over to Yankee Stadium, just about every day. It was about twelve miles from where we lived. His father worked there. Frankie

got to see all the Yankee games free.
Now, on this particular day, Frankie and I, was kicking ass, and taking names. I recall, on one play, I had the ball, and was looking around for Frankie. I looked, and he had two sewers on the other team. So, I reared back, and let the ball fly. Frankie saw the ball, but he didn't see the vegetable wagon coming up the block. He was headed straight for it.

I yelled, "look out, Frankie". He didn't hear me. As he reached for the ball, he ran dead into the wagon, and fell. We all ran to see what had happened to Frankie. When we got there, he was holding his foot, moaning and groaning. I thought to myself. It was my fault, and I probably fucked up Frankie's running career. I felt like shit. The rest of the cats were not concerned about Frankie being hurt. They were only glad that he didn't catch the ball. They didn't give a shit about Frankie. But I did. As it turned out, he only scraped his ankle. That's all.
Later on, Frankie graduated from James Monroe High School in the Bronx. He went to NYU, and became a member of the track team. He ran the mile race. I recall, seeing him, when he won the Wanamaker Mile at the Garden. Boy, did I feel good.

My father moved again. This time he bought a house in Jamaica, Queens. It was different.

No more flights of stairs to climb. No vestibules to hang out in. No roof to play on. No fire escapes. My sisters had their room, I had mine. My father finally got a day gig in the Post Office. My mother didn't have yell at me and my sisters anymore. I had finished junior high school in the Bronx. I went to Jamaica High School. I met a cat named Walter Johnson Jr. Everybody called him, Junnie. He played the drums. His father played drums for the Fletcher Henderson Orchestra. One of the great band leaders and arrangers of his time. In fact, Fletcher did a bunch of arrangements for the Benny Goodman Orchestra.

I spent a lot of time down in Junnie's basement, listening to jazz records. Junnie played the drums while listening to the records. I told him I always wanted to play the trumpet. Especially, after hearing Louis Armstrong. Junnie had an old beat up trumpet that he gave me. I was able to blow it.

I started to taking lessons from a cat who played for the Claude Hopkins Orchestra.

He dug the grape. But when he was straight, he taught me some pretty hip licks. All I had to do, was bring him a

taste, every now and then.
One day some cats came by
Junnie's basement. One cat had a tenor
sax. Another cat, had an alto sax. And
the other cat had a bass. We started to
jam, and if I do say so myself, we sounded
pretty good. After about six months of
jammin', we decided to form a band. We
found a cat who played some funky piano.
We played some gigs at the local
community center, every Saturday night,
and at other clubs in the area. Everybody
dug us. Everybody said we sounded just
like the Savoy Sultans. Now man, that was
one hell of a compliment. The Savoy Sultans
was the house band at the Savoy Ballroom
in Harlem. It was called the home of happy
feet.
The Savoy Ballroom featured the
Battle of the Bands. All the big bands came
to the Savoy for the battle.

'The Sultans put a hurtin' on any band
that took them on in battle. Didn't make
any difference who they were, or their
reputation. The Sultan's blew them away.
After a few gigs, I was able to buy
me a horn. Not a new one, but a pretty
good one. At least I didn't have to keep it
together with rubber bands. I bought it at
a pawn shop, on Park Row.
I was beginning to get my chops

in shape. All the cats said, I had a pretty
good sound. I practiced a lot down in
Junnie's basement. My father did not
allow me to blow my horn at home. It
always puzzled me, why my father didn't
dig my wanting to be in show business.
After all, he had two sisters in
show business. My mother had two brothers
who could tap their ass off. They all played
on Broadway, the Apollo, Lafayette Theatres,
Connies Inn, the Cotton Club. I recall, sitting
on the steps in the balcony of the theatres,
watching some of the great Black performers
Case in point.

Bert Williams, Ethel Waters,
Maude Russell, Jackie (Moms) Mabley,
(the funniest woman in the world). The Big
Bands of: Jimmie Lunceford, Tiny Bradshaw,
Lucky Millinder, and Jazz Royalty…The Duke,
and The Count. Some of the greatest tap
dancers, The Nicholas Brothers, Pete, Peaches
and Duke, Tip, Tap and Toe. And one hell of a
tap dancer, Teddy Hale, and many, many more.
I spent most of my time jammin' down
in Junnie's basement. I never made the big time.
I just blew.

1940-1949 "Hip" Recollections
POETICALLY
Expressed

Perplexed…Out of Context…What's Next!
(Ass Kickin' Time)

I made it through the twenties and the
thirties without too much pain.
But, in the forties…………
Profane. Insane……………………

Like, some cat named Hitler.
Goin' 'round kickin' ass…no class.
Mussolini…another jive ass cat.
Japan with the sneak attack…………

Man, that's when the shit hit the fan.
Uncle Sam pointing his finger at me.
Making me feel guilty.
So, I signed up for the scene.

Served 3 1/2 years of mean.
Taking mucho crap.
Sure turning my cheek after each slap.
I did wish I had my druthers.

'Cause a lotta cold shit came down
on the brothers…
Having to "pee" in the colored latrine.
Same routine…Water Fountain.

Mess Hall…anywhere you went at all.
Being called "you people" even if you
were alone. That cut through to the bone.
Our Military Occupational Specialty. MOS

Truck Drivers. Port Battalion. Cooks.
Bakers. No more. No less. So, I never
got to fight the enemy.
I was confused anyway as to "who he be"?

I was just plain "Old Black GI Joe" below
the Mason-Dixon line. No fault of mine.
I wondered. Did I wear a different uniform?
The way I was treated, and scorned.

But, I got an honorable discharge for
services rendered.
And thought to myself.
Has this shit really ended?

Veterans from New York got 52-20.
(A bonus of $20 bucks for 52 weeks)
It wasn't shit. It helped a bit. Put some
loot in my slide. While I tried.

To get my head together, for whatever.
I still dug the trumpet. Loved "Pops" and
Jazz. He had the true sound of brass. But,
I couldn't cut it like I wanted to.

So, my blowing days were through.
And, somehow I just knew.
Jazz was the music for me.
And it would always be.

Then I met Helen…a real foxy chick.
I drew a bead on her…real quick.
We dug each other.
After awhile…boogied down the aisle.

Had two kids. Avoided the skids. Used
my GI Bill like everyone had, and bought
a brand new pad. Living good in a new
neighborhood. Wyandanch, Long Island.

1940-1949 Recollections JAZZFULLY Expressed

I recall, sitting in the Carlton Theatre in Jamaica, with some of the cats from the band. We were digging Andy Kirk and his Twelve Clouds of Joy. They were swinging like crazy. He had two great singers in the band. A cat by the name of Phe Terrel, and a chick June Richman. In the band also, was the incomparable piano player, Mary Lou Williams. The cats and I were really enjoying the show.

All of a sudden the house lights came up, and some cat walked out on stage and announced. "The Japanese have just bombed Pearl Harbor". We all looked at each other. I said, "where the fuck is that". President Roosevelt straightened me out with his radio broadcast. He not only told me where it was at, but that it was an act of war.

The weeks that followed was a bitch.

My family split up. My mother and one sister went to work in Washington, D.C. My other sister was in boarding school, somewhere in New Jersey. My father and I were the only ones at home. He still had his gig in the Post Office. I had a bullshit job in Long Island City.

The band broke up. Most of the cats had been drafted. I began to hang out with some of my homies from the Bronx. We decided to go down to Whitehall Street and enlist. We were going to be drafted pretty soon anyway.

A couple of days before we were to go, I came down with an impacted wisdom tooth. It was a muthfucka. I didn't make it. I felt like shit. I felt even worse, after seeing the picture in the Daily News of the cats with Joe Louis. He was there to sign up the same day. I should have been there.

After I got straight with the wisdom tooth, me and two of my friends from the Bronx (Jack and Bennie) enlisted. We were inducted at Camp Upton, Long Island.

Jack and I were sent to Camp Lee, Virginia. Bennie went to some camp in Louisanna. We had never been that far away from the Bronx.

I recall, Jack and I arrived to Camp Lee at night. It was raining like hell. We were left standing in the rain for quite awhile. One thing I noticed. When the GI overcoat got wet, it smelled like shit. I'll never forget the Sergeant that greeted us. I'll also never forget the first thing he said. He said, "the one thing I can't stand, is a half/ass soldier". It didn't take me long to

figure out just what he meant.
Camp Lee was where I received my basic training, which was learning how to drive the 6x6 Army trucks. I passed all the tests, and became a qualified driver. The most important and necessary skill, was your ability to drive in a convoy, and especially at night. Now, that was a bitch.
During our training, we had many recreational activities.

I tried out for the boxing team. You got a break from "KP" if you were on the team. But, the first time some cat hit me in my mouth, I said, "no way, I ain't gonna fuck up my chops".
The special services unit was holding auditions for a show. It was called "Blackouts of 1942". The producer was a cat, Paul Ash. He used to be the leader of the pit band at the Roxy Theatre in New York City. Jack and I auditioned for a part in the show. It was called the Onyx Club Revue. It was the part of the show, the "colored soldiers" could get a part. Jack and I wrote a song, "The Rifle Range Song".
Everybody dug it.
When I completed my training, I was sent to Denver, Colorado, up in the damn mountains. I had a hell of a time breathing, the air was so fuckin'

thin. Nothing like the air in the Bronx.
And man, it was as cold as a whore's
Heart.

I became a Sergeant, and was in
charge of the Motor Pool. After about a
year and half, I was accepted to attend
Officers Candidate Infantry School at
Fort Benning, Georgia. You graduated
as a Second Lieutenant in the Infantry.
A 90 day wonder. Just before I left, the
cats were shipped overseas to drive
convoy for the Red Ball Express.
Now, Officers Candidate School
was a different scene, as far as the way I
was treated. No more "for colored only",
except if you took the bus to town, and had
to sit in the back. No separate mess hall,
barracks or latrine. I felt pretty good. I
began to believe that I was one of the cats.
I recall, I was on a break from one
of the field problems. I was standing by a
fence with two cats from my platoon. They
were white. There was only five brothers
who started class with me. They washed out
in the first six weeks. In fact, I just made it.
We were smoking and talking, when this
farmer walks over, joins the conversation.

Asking, where we're from, and lots of
other miscellanious shit. The cats all
answered, and I felt free to have some

input. Which I did.

All of a sudden he stops. Looks at me, funny like. I said to myself, "oh shit, here it comes". I'd heard that Georgia cats can be some mean ass muthas, when it came to dealing with the brothers.

He said to me, as he squinted his eyes, and scratched his balls. "Oh, you one of them smart ass Niggers from up North, and I guess you think you're somebody, don't you? Well, I may be an old country bumpkin, and don't know shit from shinola. But, I can take off these overalls, get a shave and a haircut, put on a shirt and tie, and I can run for President of the United States. That's one thing you could never do, smart as you think you are".

I didn't respond like he thought I would.

I didn't scratch my head, bow down or shuffle my feet. He was pissed. So was I. But, the sick son of a bitch, told the natural truth. The significance of that remark stayed with me for a long, long time.

Well, with two weeks to go before graduation, I fell in a gopher hole, while carrying a tripod for a 50 millimeter machine gun, during a field problem. An Infantry Company in attack. Our final field problem. I busted up my ankle pretty bad. I was in the hospital for a long time. While in the hospital, they discovered that my ear drums had been perforated. Probably from the muzzle blast of an anti-tank gun, while giving the firing orders.

That was it. I had been fitted for my officers uniform, and had planned to join the 555 (triple nickle) parachute division. It was the only Black parachute outfit. My gung-ho, was no mo! Classified limited duty, I finished my tour of duty at, Fort Bragg, North Carolina.

Was discharged at Fort Dix, New Jersey. February 6th, 1946. Then home. Guess where? THE BRONX.

1950-1969 "Hip" Recollections Poetically Expressed

Suburban Pioneers…More Fears…Shifting Gears…"Lord Knows I Tried"

In the fifties and sixties things started to happen…no time for nappin'. The Do Do had hit the fan. Man! Folk opened their eyes, realized, recognized, summarized.

"Hey, how 'bout a piece of the pie" was the cry. "We done paid our dues, we tired of bad news. Time to move on. We've been half-stepping too long".

Things got started kind of slow. Shit, we didn't know how the game was played. But, we stayed, prayed. And bit by bit the pieces began to fit.

New voices were heard spreading the word. Malcolm was the loudest. The proudest. His message was emphatic. Dramatic! Not easy to accept.

But that was X.
His word had gotten out.
Time to shout…say it loud.
"I'm Black and I'm Proud".

Along came Dr. King's thing.
"Move on" "No turning back"
"We are all brothers" Black
Panther's didn't dig that shit.

Time to hit…them muthas!
Angela…Stokley…Rapp…Adam.
Up and at 'em. Like white on
rice…no matter the price.

I got caught up in the movement.
Spent quality time in the community.
Subsequently, became the main man
for the War On Poverty program.

"Burn Baby Burn" the word that was
heard. "Black Power" was the call for all
to pay attention…not to mention.
Demonstrations…scary situations.

I tried to get the folk together for
whatever. Most of the time it was sad…
bad as it could get…and yet sometimes
it was good…the community would………

Cooperate, graduate to a higher plane.
Like when we became involved and elected
a Black to the school board. Started moving
toward self-determination and concentration.

Now, I for one to get the job done.
Kept the shit stirred up…just enough
to keep the folk on the case. To erase
the crabs in a basket syndrome.

A destructive characteristic practiced
by some. The changes were tough…
rough…but really light stuff. Check out
our history…it ain't no mystery.

We would survive…stay alive.
Kickin'…Stickin…Takin' a Lickin'…
Every now and then.
So, listen up friend.

I'd like to thank my friend Max.
Who came up with the theme. It's
mean…hits with a clout. Check it out!
I am the Lord. Thy God. I Am. That I Am.

For the sins they committed at Treblinka
For the four little girls in Birmingham.
For those at Auchwitz and Watts who died.
The heavens darkened. And Jesus cried.

For the six million who died guiltless.
For the damnable fiasco called Viet Nam.
For the Civil, Human Rights still denied.
The heavens darkened. And Jesus cried.

For the pettiness, smugness of Egomania.
For those who think they know. They don't!
For Facism and Racism that stays alive.
The heavens darkened. And Jesus cried.

For the loss of childhood dreams and magic.
For the smell of fear that embodies our soul.
For Dr. King and Ghandi who tried.
The heavens darkened. And Jesus cried.

For the hating & killing that won't go away
For Armageddon, that's so close at hand.
For the good, the love that won't survive.
The heavens darkened. And Jesus cried.

I AM THE LORD. THEY GOD. I AM.
THAT I AM. THAT I AM!!

1950-1969 RECOLLECTIONS JAZZFULLY EXPRESSED

I finally got a gig in the Post Office. Like father like son, I guess. The bread wasn't shit, but it was steady. My father and I made a deal. I used my GI Bill to buy a house in, Jamaica, Queens. He loaned me the down payment.

My mother and father were now living in my house. My youngest sister and her husband moved in with their two boys. My other sister was straight, she married a doctor. My daughter was born, and the ten of us lived together. We had the room. Stayed out of each others way, and everything was cool.

I recall, that my mother had a gig at a real estate office. One day she came home, and told me about an interracial housing development on Long Island. It was in a town called, Wyandanch. Now, if you were hip, you knew interracial was just another way of saying "Blacks Only"

It was called George Washington Carver Homes. Need I say more?
Helen and I went out to Wyandanch. We checked out the models. Dug 'em. Decided to buy one. We sold the house in Jamaica. My father had retired. He and my mother moved to a place of their own. My

sister and her husband, also bought a home. Everybody was straight. So, Helen and I moved to Wyandanch.

We had a three bedroom home on a corner lot. It was a new adventure, and a real exciting time for Helen and the kids. It was not only exciting, but demanding as well. No street lights. No paved streets. No garbage pick-up, and only one school. Owning a home on Long Island, was a brand new scene for all the cats and their families, who bought a home in Wyandanch.

Everybody needed a car to go anywhere, and especially to work. Most of the cats had a gig in the City. The "A" train wasn't available, and no buses were running. We were all in the same boat.

The mortgages were all held by the same bank. All the houses looked alike. You found out who could keep your car running. Who could fix things around the house. Who kept the top drawer booze? One thing that happened quite often, was when somebody got drunk, and couldn't find their house. Like I said, all the houses looked alike, so you never knew who would just walk in. We had one cat in the neighborhood, who did that shit all the time.

Helen got used to walking the kids back and forth to school. And I driving back and forth to work. I still worked in the Post

Office in Jamaica. It was about 35 miles one way. It wasn't too bad. The parkway was near, and took me right to where I worked. The only thing though, when it snowed, it really became a hazardous trip.

I finally got involved in the community, socially and politically. That's when the pain set in. It was a bitch. A couple of cats and I, organized a civic club, and began to hold meetings.

My friend Jack, who also had moved to Wyandanch, and I, wrote a song for the civic club. It was called, "Carver Park In The Dark". Man, we didn't realize how much in the dark we were. After a few meetings, we began to see the light. We recognized some of the things we had to deal with.

The first thing on the agenda, was another school, and like right away. It was easier said than done. The reality hit home when we found out how much bread it would cost. We also found out what we needed to do, to get the bread. It was simple. More taxes. Shit, after awhile we also found out, the only way to get anything for the community, pay more taxes. Just to get a fucking street light, we had to pay more taxes. I felt like I had just stepped off the plane, and walked dead into the propeller.

We assessed the situation, and what the deal was all about. We finally got a handle on it.

Wyandanch was a Hamlet of the Town of Babylon. I said, "no shit, what the hell does that mean". We found out in a hurry what it meant. The Town of Babylon was the local government, where we paid local taxes for local shit. And that's what we got in return. Shit!
We were politically anemic. The old taxation without representation. We didn't even have any tea, or a harbor to throw it in. All we could do, was pull our puddin'. We all agreed, something had to be done, and immediately.
In the months that followed, I had become politically active in the community. We were growing like crazy. More homes. Which translated, into more Black folk, more kids, and mucho problems. Changes were taking place all over the country. Economically, socially, politically and especially along racial lines. Black folk were pitching a bitch. The "Man" was totally confused, He had never seen Black folk raise so much hell.

The next thing we knew, along came the War On Poverty Program. The Office of Economic Opportunity. OEO.

The major thrust of the program was to pump a lot of bread, into what was identified as "poverty pockets". We were designated as one of the communities, and the Wyandanch Community Action Center was established.

I took a leave of absence from the Post Office, and was appointed Director of the Center. It didn't take me long to figure out the "hidden agenda" for the War on Poverty. The "Man", had to do something to cool out the folk. What better way to do that, than, "give 'em some money, they'll be so busy fucking it up, they won't have any time for raising hell".

It was a planned strategy that worked most of the time. But, I made it my business to research, analyze, comply with the OEO rules and regulations. I knew ain't no way you can rob the bank, unless you get inside.

With the center staff, and interested folk from the community, we got inside, and started to get our shit together.

The Center began to make an impact. A lot of it, was made possible by my staff. Especially, one lady. Amy James. Amy was a mother, grandmother, a sensitive caring person. She was always ready and willing to advocate for the folk. However, she was a lady you didn't fuck with. She'd

lay a muthfucka on you in a minute, and at
the same time take care of your problem.
I'd sic Amy on anybody who I thought was
giving us a snow job.
I recall, Amy and I met with one of
the Town political leaders, about a problem
we thought he could help us with. After, we
explained it, he began to tell us what he
could do to help us. After, listening to a lot
of "shuckin' and jivin", Amy finally had to
lay it on him. She told him, "Listen, I haven't
come here for you to pee on my leg, and then
tell me I ain't wet. Can you help us or not?
If not, stop pulling my chain".

You better believe we got down to the
nitty-gritty. We got the answers we
wanted. That was Amy. I loved her.
In a community of approximately
15,000 folk, we had more groups than
Carter had liver pills. The welfare folk.
The bourgeois and the jive ass folk
who didn't give a fuck. One way or the
other I had to turn that shit around.
I came up with a new idea. A
brand new philosophical approach. I
embraced a "modus operandi", that
worked for me. It was two pronged. "Kiss
Ass, Kick Ass". It was the centerpiece,
for what I so affectionately and lovingly
called, "ghettomatics". It didn't mean
shit. But, it sounded pretty hip.

I spent a lot of time kissing White folk ass. Especially, the powers to be at Town Hall. It took a lot of kicking ass, to get the Black folk fired up politically. We finally found our political arena, when we ran a Brother for the school board in Wyandanch.

With some of the more progressive cats in the community, we put together a political action committee, to plan a strategy.

After much street action, and meetings, the community elected a Black to the school board. In fact, every election after that, the community elected a Black to the board. It didn't take long for the complexion of the board to change. 99% of the students were Black. The board hired many Black teachers, administrators. They succeeded in implementing a very viable, and much needed curriculum.

The school board meetings became the "sounding board" for the folk. I recall, at one of the meetings, one lady was raising particular hell. She was known in the community as a real pain in the ass. I knew her. And I also knew that no one wanted to take her on, one on one. She had a lot of scars on her face, which she probably got from fighting. Everybody said, "I ain't gonna fuck with her. She must be some tough ass sister".

I said, "Shit, she ain't so tough. The one who cut her ass up, was the tough one".

My man, Ernie, was the target of her tirade. After listening to her crap, he told her if she didn't cool it, he would close the meeting.

Man, did her jaws tighten up. She looked dead at Ernie, and said. "Mr. Reynolds, if you don't listen to what I got to say. I'm gonna get up on this here table, and in a minute or two, there won't be anyone left in this room, but me. Now, munch on them grits awhile". Ernie, knew she meant every word she said, so he told her to please continue. Which she did.

I had a talk with Alma after the meeting. Like, I said, I knew her, and we got along pretty good. I asked her why she acted the way she did at the meeting. She said to me, "These damn meetings, ain't nothing but a lotta of 'Who struck John; Them and They'. Just never seem to get down to the real nitty gritty happenings goin' down in the rest of the community".

I told her things like that happen at most community meetings. Even in the White communities. But, they handle their shit a little different than we do. They keep it from stinking. She said, "I don't see how, shit stinks, no matter how you handle it".

I had to accept that. Alma and I had a very good relationship. She became one of my better community advocates. She died soon after. I really and truly, missed her.

The Center had become the listening post. The place to come to straighten out any problems you might have. With the staff and volunteers from the community, positive things started to happen.

I recall, that every Friday evening after work, I'd get together with the cats at Herb Perry's gas station. We would discuss the weekly happenings, while having a taste or two. Being, able to hold your booze, was the main requirement to participate. With, Herb, Scoog, Ernie, Ham and other interested cats, the sessions became the Genesis for most of the community services.

The Wyandanch Recognition Day Parade, which became an annual event. The organizing of the first Black Kiwanis club in Suffolk County. Because of our membership, Herb Perry and I, was able to get one of the major banks in Suffolk County to open a branch in Wyandanch.

The Kiwanis Club operated and financed the Martin Luther King Jr. ambulance corps. We certainly needed one. The ambulance outside usually got lost on a call to Wyandanch. The club was the recipient of the New York State Kiwanis

Governors Award for our ambulance project. It was a great achievement for our club, which had only been together for three years.

A health center was developed by a citizen's committee, with the help of the Center's resources. The health center was supported and operated by one of the major hospitals in the area. The majority of the employees were from the community. Amy James with her committee, their effort to build a Day Care Center became a reality.

The tree of togetherness planted by the Center, was beginning to bear fruit.

I recall, one day the staff and I were taking applications for jobs at the new A&P supermarket. A result of the Center staff, with a coordinated effort from John Wickcliffe. John Wickcliffe worked for the Amsterdam News in Harlem, and had made the original request to the A&P executives. After John and I met with the executives they agreed to open a store in Wyandanch.

However, I wasn't feeling up to par the day we were taking applications for jobs. I called the health center, and asked could I come over. They said, the doctor had not arrived as yet, but they would call when he did. They called in a short time. I went over. I was given a EKG. The results showed, I was having a heart attack. The doctor made arrangements for my admittance to the hospital. I couldn't believe it. I didn't have any chest pains.

The ambulance was out on a call.
The cat who worked as the custodian, drove me to the hospital. It was about ten miles. Like, I said, I had no chest pains. But, the way that cat drove, brought on some pain. He was steady getting up. Blowing his horn, exceeding the speed limit. He kept telling me, "don't worry you're in good hands". I thought if I'm not having a heart attack, I damn sure will have one by the time this cat gets me to the hospital.
I arrived safely. I was diagnosed with an acute myocardial infarction. I didn't know what the hell that was. I was put in the intensive care unit. Now, that was pretty scary. However, the doctor laid the good news on me. No surgery. I stayed in the hospital for 21 days. Taking mucho tests, and a lot of medication. When discharged, the doctor told me to take it easy. Watch my diet, and weight, and to make sure that I take my medication. Which I did.

I cooled out for awhile, after which I went back to work.
The Center was still going strong.

The staff was TCB (taking care of business). While in the hospital, I had thought about a lot of new ideas, and programs. One of the ideas, was to establish a Community Development Corporation. It would function as a quasi-local government. I ran the idea by our local Congressman. He thought it was a great idea. He offered to help. He helped alright. He helped himself to the idea.

It became a national program, and one of the programs under the OEO umbrella. I laid the idea on some of the cats in the community. After a few soul searching seminars at Herb Perry's gas station, the Wyandanch Community Development Corporation (WCDC), was established. A concerted effort was made to assemble those interested, to serve as members on the WCDE board of directors.

With a broad based representation of church, school and active community leaders, the WCDC began to go to work.

The first order of business, was an effort to build a housing development. A much needed facility. After, many, and I mean many meetings, a plan was put into motion. We involved Black businesses, contractors, architects in the project. We received financial aid from the State. We really had high hopes. The tough gig was yet to come. Getting the support from the community.

I recall, going to a meeting to explain the project. The meeting was being held by some of the more affluent residents. My intention was to bring into focus the thrust of the program. How it would impact the community, politically, economically and socially.

Their hue and cry was, "we don't want any low-income housing project in our community. It will only bring them in with all their children, drugs and crime. All it will do for us, is raise our taxes, and cause us to build more schools. I don't think we're ready, or need any housing project".

I really became pissed. Not so much for their concern about the schools, and the taxes. But, the reference to "them". I said, "if you're worried about "them", I got news for you. As far as Town Hall, and the powers to be, all of us is "THEM". That statement from me, caused some abusive verbal comments toward me. I realized my attendance was no longer necessary. So, I booked.

The meeting helped me to recognize the unpleasant, disturbing aspect of some folk moral considerations. It didn't matter anyway. Town Hall fucked us. They turned down our zoning request. If the request had been approved the bulldozers were ready to move the next day. I cried. The Center staff, the WCDC board of directors, were literally sick to their stomachs, and very, very angry.

After the shock wave passed, we returned to our regular gig, working for the betterment of the community. The Center was on full speed ahead, and the staff had found their groove. It was time for another project. Just what I needed. If you believe.

It was becoming evident, that the government was backing away from the War on Poverty. It all began, when President Nixon tried to kill the program, but was stopped by the court. The bread and support became hard to come by. I figured what we needed to do, was to put in place our own government.

I inquired and read about the possibility of Wyandanch becoming an incorporated Town. After much research, incorporation seemed like the answer to our problem. Not all, but many of them.

The area to be incorporated was contiguous. We had our own School District. Fire District. Postal District. Election Districts. A major roadway, and the Long Island Railroad, were an important part of the community. I was able to get a student from Stony Brook University, to conduct a feasibility study for me. In the meantime I had talked up the idea with some of the hip and active cats in the community. They all agreed to participate.

When the study was over, we organized as a committee on incorporation. We met religiously, and discussed the pros and cons. We finally agreed, that we should move on. We went to Albany, and met with the office responsible for all the legal ramifications of incorporation.

They read our feasibility study, and listened to our reasons. They concluded that we should proceed. They wished us success, and offered to help. We left with pamphlets, booklets containing all the information we would need.

We held many, and again, many meetings to read and discuss, what we needed to do. Two things had to happen. We needed the Town approval, and the community had to vote. The Town was all in favor. What better way, to get us off their back?

Now, to tell the folk about the incorporation, and what it would mean, was another tough gig. Once again, it was that haunting refrain, "community diversity".

It was a bitch. For months the committee and I went on a selling spree. We visited with folk, who we felt would be interested. Church leaders, Town politicians, folk who had a certain sphere of influence, anybody who would listen to us.

Finally, a public hearing was held.
The stage was set. The folk got the opportunity to express their opinions, pro and con. It was six hours of "rhetorical diarrhea". In other words, folk talked shit for days. But, that's what it was all about. Folk letting it all "hang out". The record of the hearing was compiled by the chairman, a local judge. It was submitted to the Town board of supervisors. They agreed to place the proposal on the next scheduled voting ballot.
While waiting for the vote, a lotta shit was going on. Not only in Wyandanch, but in the whole Town of Babylon. The same 'ol same 'ol. Everybody promoting their own agenda. I was getting frustrated with all the EGO trippin' taking place in Wyandanch.

I was getting tired of "fattening frogs for snakes" and "goin' to the meetin'. Somebody asked me, "what'd I find out at all them meetings"? I told him, "shit, the only thing I find out, is when the next meetings gonna be".
Most of my enthusiasm had gradually begun to fade. However, I still directed all my energy, and time toward making the Incorporation of Wyandanch a reality. The Town had not acted on our referendum. The support for the proposal had started to dwindle. I suspected the

Town politicians, after serious thought, and recognizing the economic, and political clout we would obtain, had second thoughts.

I knew that was the case, after talking to one of the Town Board members, who I thought was in our corner. I'll never forget what he said to me. "You know your proposal is very good, but it seems to be somewhat ambitious, or maybe, it's just not the time for something like that".

I knew right away, that we were dead in the water. The proof of that was, the referendum never came up for a vote. Once again the Town had fucked us. And once again I cried. I really and truly believed, if we had become a self-governing entity, it would have been a most meaningful, and historical accomplishment. Of all the disappointments I had experienced, this one hurt the most.

In the months that followed, the OEO was under constant fire from the Congress. It looked like the War On Poverty, had been lost. It was over.

I felt good about the hard work, and dedication of my staff, and the involvement of the concerned community folk. Now, regardless, of the constant bullshit, the perverse activity of the poverty pimps, and the lame ass excuses, we still implemented many successful programs.

We might not have won the war, but we kicked the shit out of those who took us on in battle. I took a little time out. Spent more time with Helen and the kids.

She was a lot happier. She told all of our friends, that I had finally given up my mistress. Wyandanch. No question about it. I loved every bit of my involvement. The Folk. The Community.

1970-1979 "HIP" RECOLLECTIONS POETICALLY EXPRESSED

"Ain't Nothin' Else To Do But Swing"

Now, the seventies and eighties put a hurtin'
on me. Especially Watergate
taking center stage. And that crap called Rock
and Roll all the rage.

I've heard it said. Music hath charm to soothe
the savage beast. But, take it from me most
"expoobidently". The so-called music of today,
just agitates the beast. To say the least.

What I'd like to know.
Where did the music go?
What happened to Moon and June?
To Melody and Harmony.

To singers who sing on key.
Eighteen cats playing together musically.
Good music feels right at home, as it always
has in JAZZ. Charlie Parker!!

Man, you ain't never heard anybody play
like him…Jim!
He was the "Bird" soaring with grace
along his own musical path.

Withstanding the wrath of those
who didn't dig his playing.
But, I'm saying. "Bird" was a genius
for innovation…improvisation.

Which he took to task, and never asked
for anything in return.
Man, he could really burn.
Diz and Monk had eyes.

'Cause they realized, "Bird" was a
phenom…an icon.
A cat who actually, in reality
Distinguished himself.

Because he rejected the accepted
language of Jazz.
It wasn't for the barrooms…
or For Dancers Only.

It was a music to be listened to.
And he knew.
It would be difficult to do.
But, he blew!

With cats like Diz, Monk, Max and
Miles hangin' on. "Bird" came on
strong. They all watched him soar
looking for more musical challenges.

The demons and fears were always around trying to keep him down. "Bird" played in spite of adversity and always painted a masterpiece musically.

"Bird" died at age 34. How much more music did he have left in him. Nobody knows. To close. Let me reiterate, set the record straight... *"Bird Lives, Man" "Bird Lives"*!!

1980-1989 Recollections Jazzfully Expressed

"Ain't Nothin' To It…But To Do It"

My father died while visiting a
friend in St. Croix, U.S. Virgin Islands.
My mother had died three months
before. I called my father's friend, who
I knew. He invited me to come on down.
I figured, I could use a little R & R. So,
I went to St. Croix.
As soon as I arrived, got off the
plane, I was completely knocked out by
the weather. I really dug it. I asked a
cat at the airport about the weather. He
told me, "the mean temperature is
always between 80 to 90 degrees". I said,
"sure ain't nothing mean about that".
My fathers friend, Ralph, picked
me up at the airport, and drove to where
he lived. Didn't take me long to get hip to
the laid back Island living. A totally
different scene. I decided right then and
there. This was it!

I called Helen, and told her to
come on down, and take a look. She did.
She stayed about a week, then went back
to Long Island. I could tell, she wasn't that
excited about St. Croix. But, after a few

calls, and the kids got on her case, she reluctantly gave in. She sold the house, the car, and came on down. She arrived with all our worldly goods in cardboard boxes. She said she had cried all the way down.

I had met a cat named Stan, who was in real estate. We became friendly, and after a few rounds of golf, he sold me a home, and Helen and I moved in. We settled in, and began a whole new life style and experience.

I became interested in the Island happenings. Like what else? It turned out to be nothing new for me. I found out things weren't that much different for the folk, than what I had to deal with in Wyandanch. The same root problems. Poverty, politics, social and economic ills. Hell, I was back in my comfort zone.

The culture was predicated on a strong birthright syndrome, that was augmented by an overwhelming ethnic diversity. It wasn't the kind of shit a cat from the Bronx, had any business sticking his nose into. But, I needed a gig.

I finally was hired by the Virgin Island OEO program, as Community Information Officer. Where else? I just thought it might be different. It wasn't. Same 'ol shit (SOS). It was compounded by the geographical complexities. The U.S. Virgin Islands consists of three

Islands, St. Thomas, St. John and St. Croix. Each Island had it's own agenda.
Sounded familiar.
I worked for the program for about a year. I couldn't handle it. Had to give it up. I wasn't ready for another heart attack. Helen got a gig with the Island Health Department. She dug it. Who wouldn't. Twenty-seven holidays.
I met a cat named Roy. His parents were from St. Croix.

He became my running buddy. He showed me where the bodies were buried. Hipped me to who was who. Something I found out, you really needed to know.
I went back to work in the Post Office. I had reinstatement privilege, because of my service disability. I only had to complete three more years, I already had served twenty-seven years, plus age, to become eligible. Believe me, the three years was a bitch.
I had to deal with the Island work ethics, and culture.
I recall, one evening Helen and I were invited by some folk we had just met. When we arrived, we rang the doorbell, and they opened the door. The first thing they said to us was, "Goodnight". Now that blowed

my mind. We had just got there, and already they were saying goodnight. I asked "what's with the goodnight".

They explained, in the evening they say, "Good Night", just like in the morning they say, "Good Morning". Both mean the same thing. "Have a Good Morning", and "Have a Good Night". It made sense to me and Helen. I began to get into the rhythm and groove of the Island folk.

After I retired, I had one hell of a retirement party. Cats came down from Wyandanch, and the Bronx. Many friends from St. Croix also attended. The party lasted one whole week. Going to the beach. Sight seeing, and having a taste or two. Booze was no problem. In fact, the tonic water cost more than the Vodka. Everybody had a ball.

When the cats cut out, I spent most of my time just "chillin". The beach and playing golf. I had a gig at the golf course at the Buccaneer Hotel. I worked every Thursday afternoon for Tim Johnston. The golf pro. He played with the heavy hitters at Fountain Valley, for some bread.

I was responsible for scheduling tee times, selling golf accessories, turning in the bread, and closing shop. I wasn't paid a salary, but I played all the free golf

I wanted. I played with a group of golfing cats. Howie, Louie, Gene and Rocky. Tim called us, The Soul Patrol, The Awesome Foursome. We were good.
I was living it up.
But, it didn't take long before I became involved again. I met this lady, who was in charge of a social program, administered by The Catholic Diocese of The Virgin Islands. It was called, The Christian Community Conscious Center (CCCC). I told her about my previous experience and she suggested that I might be interested in doing some volunteer work. I told her, I wasn't of the Catholic faith, and would that make a difference. She said no. So, naturally I agreed to do it.
It didn't take long before I became the Executive Director of the program.

Here I was, once again knee-deep into the shit. I had no trepidations about the gig. It was a familiar ballpark for me. But, I found out right away, the rules and the players were different. Once again it took awhile, to get hip to the Crucian culture, and personality of the St. Croix folk. After a concerted effort to understand, and working with the folk, I got the job done.
I stayed with the program for about five years. While there, I became president of the St. Croix Chapter of the AARP. The

president of the St. Croix Jazz Society. Helen and I became members of the Courtyard Players, a theater company. We acted in plays. I wrote and directed some of the productions. I was a busy cat, for someone retired. I'd heard that retirement can be hazardous to your health, if all you did was sit on your ass. However, doing too much, wasn't cool either.

What I really dug the most, was my involvement in the St. Croix Jazz Society. Jazz was my soulmate.

I recall, with some of the cats, we produced the first Caribbean Jazz Summit. We had cats come from the different Islands to St. Croix, and jam. The venue was the beach at St. Croix by the Sea. A local hotel.

It was outta sight!

I really believed Helen and I would spend the rest of our lives living on St. Croix. Why not? Living on an Island in the Caribbean, wasn't suppose to be happening to some cat from the Bronx. Lots of sandy beaches. Never more than fifteen minutes from a beach, no matter where you were. St. Croix is the only Island in the Caribbean, that is completely surrounded by the Caribbean Sea. Trade winds blowing, just when you needed it. Palm trees, swaying in the breeze. Not too shabby. Not too shabby, at all. And the bottom line. Ain't nobody in a hurry. If you ask someone to do something right away. The answer. "We'll

hurry up, and do it tomorrow".
All this came to a screeching halt in September 1989.
Hurricane Hugo ripped St.
Croix apart.

The winds reached over 200 miles an hour. Helen and I rode the storm out at a friends house. It was suppose to be what they call a "safe" house. I said, "no shit, the way that wind is blowing, ain't nothing safe". From 10PM, until the next morning. Hurricane Hugo, stomped, and kicked the shit out of St. Croix.
We spent the whole night, praying and crying. Listening to the wind, rain and glass breaking. Seemed like morning would never come. When morning finally came, I looked outside. It looked like the Planet of the Apes. It was an unbelievable sight. Nothing was where it once was. Everything that was green, was no more. Rooftops were strewn all over the landscape. It was a good thing it struck at night, and everybody stayed inside. The metal roofs were flying around like frisbees. It wasn't smart, or safe to be outside. My friend looked outside and shouted. "Where the hell is the house that was next door. It ain't there anymore. It's gone. I mean, it's gone"!!

Right then and there, I knew our prayers had been answered. We were still here. The house was still

here.
Three days later, things seemed
to have calmed down. Helen and I
decided to go home. My car had not been
damaged. The drive home usually took me
only about fifteen minutes. However, when
I started to drive, I immediately became
disoriented. I had made that trip, I don't
know how many times, in the fourteen
years I had lived on St. Croix. But, now I
didn't recognize any landmarks at all.
None. Nothing was were it used to be. It
was scary. Downright spooky.
Driving very carefully for about
three hours, I arrived to where we lived.
Or should I say, where we used to live.
The whole area was devastated.
Every home was damaged. Some completely
destroyed. We made it to our house. We
saw that the front door was still intact.
We didn't have much damage. I thought.

When I opened the door, I immediately
saw how wrong I was.
I could see right out the back. No
back. The sides were blown away. No roof.
Actually, all that was left, was the front
door. The inside was a total mess. The
furniture, fixtures were all thrown around.
The floor was covered with water. It's hard
to believe, but not one of my Jazz albums,
had fallen off the shelves, or damaged. I
knew then, that GOD, loved Jazz.

The aftermath was a bitch. It wasn't like in school, "after math comes English". It was all about survival. No power. No water. No gas. Most of the stores, did not have any food. Above all, no law and order. We were cut off from everybody. No communication. Not able to contact family and friends, on or off the Island. Helen and I had to bunk with her mother. She lived in a senior citizen complex, that hadn't suffered much damage. She had a one bedroom apartment. It was definitely close quarters.

It was very hard to deal with, but we had to make it work. We did, until we decided what we were going to do. The first thing, I submitted our claim to the insurance company. The adjuster, then appraised the property as a total lost. We received a check for 100% of the policy coverage. We were very fortunate. Most of the insurance companies on Island bellied up on the folk. It was a stone cold fucking drag, and incomprehensible. I made up my mind, right then and there. We had to get the hell off St. Croix. Helen agreed. Which was hard for her to do. She loved St. Croix. Now, where to go? I damn sure wasn't going back to the Bronx, or any where, with cold ass weather. All the

years in the Caribbean, it had to be some
place warm.
We finally decided to move to
Florida. I wasn't ready for that.

I recall, back in the forties, when
I was still playing trumpet. Some ofay cat
asked me if I'd like to play a gig with him
in Miami. I told him, hell no. He said, "why"?
I told him, 'man, that's your Ami...not Miami!!
Nevertheless, we finally moved to Florida. Now,
that's another story.

1990-MILLENIUM "HIP" RECOLLECTIONS
POETICALLY
EXPRESSED

I'm not over the hill-Just on the back nine
"Growin' Old Ain't For Sissies"

Like, I'm eighty-one.
Which ain't no big deal. What counts man,
is how you feel. Shit, life's a bitch, no
matter how much you dig it...

My journey so far has been a bitch.
Which, shouldn't come as any surprise.
I never won the big prize.
Had my ups. Had my downs.

Dealing with clowns.
Testing Fate. Staying Straight.
Slipping. Sliding. Ducking. Hiding.
But, movin' and groovin'.

Listen up, Bro'.
Something you needs to know.
Seems like all the passion and danger we once had
Has been replaced by credit cards.
Attache cases.
Compensatory time.
And a baddazz pad.

Can't let ourselves be too cool.
The "MAN'S" no fool.
The yearning for learning.
Must forever keep burning.

And remember, skin tone…alone.
Doesn't mean you're Black.
It's a state of mind
That's where it's at.

Here's something I don't understand.
And it really, really bugs me, man.
Why some folk, I guess.
Just don't dig their Blackness.

Not Me.
No Siree!
I know who I am………….
"Oo Bop Sha' Bam"………

Talk the talk. Walk the walk.
Toe tappin'. Finger snappin.
Grits & Greens. New Orleans.
Kind of Blue. My locks. My do.

Marvin Gaye. Poitier.
Quincy Jones. Neck Bones.
Motown. Gettin' down.
Bid Whist. The Twist.

Lindy Hop. BeBop.
Lennox Ave. The Harlem River View.
Thats gospel. A natural fact.
Get to that!!

The celebration of Black History month
in February. I don't think it's necessary.
Black History "IS" America's history.
In every aspect of America's legacy.

Black History is woven in the tapestry.
In spite of the adversity.
You got any doubt.
Check this out!

Frederick Douglas. W.E.B. DuBois.
Harriet Tubman. Marion Anderson.
Dr. Martin Luther King Jr. Adam Clayton
Powell Jr. Mohammed Ali. The NAACP.

Dr. Charles Drew. Thurgood Marshall.
Paul Robeson. Jackie Robinson
And finally. The Duke. The Count.
Jazz Royalty.

I think I understand the "MAN". Being "culturally anemic" about American Blacks. He allows perceptions and stereotypes to dictate the facts.

A simple answer. NOT TO KNOW IS
A CURSE................
NOT TO "WANT" TO KNOW IS
WORSE!!..................

I know their be an enemy among us.
But remember, HE had his Judas.
So like HIM hang in. Stay strong.
Keep on keepin' on. Keep on keepin' on.

But something else bothers the shit
outta me. I can't remember when there's
been this much discombobulation.
A Baddazz Situation!

Just what the fuck is goin' on.
Morn til Night. Everybody uptight.
Hating and killing for no reason.
Like it's open season.

Too much bullshit prevails.
Overcrowded jails.
BIG MAC & CRACK consumed
by the masses. Dumb asses!

Television's insatiable appetite.
Spewing out garbage, day and night.
Talk shows?
More like "squawk shows".

People bitchin' with a loaf of bread
under each arm. Sounding the alarm.
'The sky's gonna fall".
"I gotta get to the mall".

Porno, Homo…kids brutalized, sodomized,
regardless of age, sex or size. Gotta
turn up the juice on the sick muthafuckas
'runnin 'round loose.

Mixed messages designed to confuse.
What's suppose to be funny, doesn't
amuse. More for the greedy. Fuck the
needy. I got mine. You get yours.

The homeless down on all fours.
Mediocrity is acceptable. When it belongs
in the porcelain receptacle. A kick ass
culture. Addicted to a tabloid mentality.

Fuck reality. Massaging the EGO at a
rapid pace. Just in case you haven't heard.
The EGO is a jealous GOD.
That must be served.

Duke Ellington wrote a song.
"Things Ain't What They Used To Be"
For me that meant. "no mo backa da bus"
"Eat at lunch counter without a fuss".

Exercise my right of franchise.
However, some things still ain't what
they used to be. Responsibility,
respectability, morality, a strong family.

As to all of the above.
I'm guiltless.
To tell the truth. I'm scared shitless.
I know GOD, is upset with the flock.

So, if I'm walking down a block pass a
house owned by a cat named NOAH.
I'm walking slower. To see if he's
building a boat in the back.

And Jack! If he is. I'm signing up. Square
biz. 'Cause if that OZONE layer continues
to crack. Be you, Red, Yellow, Brown,
White or Black.

There won't be any need to worry about
THEM or THEY. Hey! Not even the HAVE
NOT or the HAVES. EVERYBODY'S ASS
WILL BE UP FOR GRABS!!

I know every closed eye ain't sleep. Every
goodby ain't gone. That's why I been around
this long. Keepin' my eye on the sparrow. Be
sure my opinions and views never narrow.

And at this moment and time. I've embraced a philosophy that suits me to a T. I do what I enjoy. I enjoy what I do. Check it out. It'll work for you.

If I get my two feet on the floor in the morning. The day is in trouble. If it's Sunday.
That's double-trouble.

So to close a few Darbyism's for the Bro's'............
"If you can't sleep. Don't count sheep"
COUNT BASIE!!

Everybody is equal sitting on the toilet bowl.
Ugly. Pretty. Rich. Poor. White. Black. Young or Old.

And finally, if in your travels you should meet. Folk who test the depth of the water with both feet.
Advise and counsel them. If they don't listen.

FUCK 'EM! NUFF SAID. Darby Hicks

0-595-29362-X